ELIZA GRISWOLD

WIDEAWAKE FIELD

Eliza Griswold is the recipient of the first Robert I. Friedman
Award for investigative journalism and is a New America Fellow
in Journalism at Harvard University, where she is at work on a
nonfiction book, *The Tenth Parallel*, also to be published by FSG.

WIDEAWAKE FIELD

WIDEAWAKE FIELD

ELIZA GRISWOLD

FARRAR, STRAUS AND GIROUX

NEW YORK

FARRAR, STRAUS AND GIROUX
18 West 18th Street, New York 10011

Distributed in Canada by Douglas & McIntyre Ltd.
Printed in the United States of America
Published in 2007 by Farrar, Straus and Giroux
First paperback edition, 2008

Some of these poems originally appeared, in slightly
different form, in the following publications:
"Buying Rations in Kabul," "How To," "Monkey,"
"Occupation," "Retreat," and "Tigers" in *The New Yorker*;
"Pennant" in *The Yale Review*; "Clean" in *The Paris Review*; "Bedbugs,"
"Mine," and "Modern City," in *Poetry*; "Arrest,"
"Come and See," and "Devi" in *Poetry Northwest*.

The Library of Congress has cataloged the hardcover edition as follows:
Griswold, Eliza, [date]
     Wideawake field / Eliza Griswold. —1st ed.
         p.   cm.
     ISBN-13: 978-0-374-29930-9 (alk. paper)
     ISBN-10: 0-374-29930-7 (alk. paper)
     I. Title.

PS3607.R58W53 2007
811'.6—dc22

                                        2006032056

Paperback ISBN-13: 978-0-374-53130-0
Paperback ISBN-10: 0-374-53130-7

www.fsgbooks.com

1 3 5 7 9 10 8 6 4 2

The author would like to thank the Corporation of Yaddo
for its generosity and support.

CONTENTS

+

WIDEAWAKE FIELD

PRINCE OF THE DOLOMITES

In a gondola above the Dolomites,
I turned to you and said, "You are
my reason for being alive." The high wire
shook. The fog that had hung
all day between the two shale crags
lifted, more like shifted toward the peaks
or what might have been the peaks
as I never saw them that day
and not ever again.

PENNANT

Love was the illusion,
the tent on the beach
with an ivory peak
that said you're never alone.
The tent is gone.
It takes you days to notice.
No pennant sings from the hill,
no slip of bright everlasting
pretends to be home. The last night comes.
The bald dunes sleep. The pilot fish leap
to bare their glistering skin.

SADNESS

When the power went off at the hotel bar,
loneliness hung between us,
not shared exactly.
The lights came on. Back then
one could smoke. I held
my drink with both hands.
I was okay. On the way home,
I bought my husband a seascape:
smudged bluffs and a boy's red
trunks *doubled in the water*.
No sadness in it anywhere.

FLOOD

I woke to a voice within the room, perhaps
the room itself: "You're wasting this life
expecting disappointment."
I packed my bag in the night
and peered in its leather belly
to count the essentials.
Nothing is essential.
To the east, the flood has begun.
Men call to each other on the water
for the comfort of voices.
Love surprises us.
It ends.

IN ANOTHER YEAR OF
FEWER DISAPPOINTMENTS

The minor angel mops his brow and laughs
his miraculous laugh, ringing with sorrow.
His face — if this is his face — this mask
of wrecked grace says, Sit with me.
Come sit with me for a while.
Ah, to be as wise as he is —

but we can't know what suffering will cost us.
It could cost the very self that longed for it,
that winked at its specter, lurking,
blueing the sky. In the wake of its coming,
the small boat of our souls —
where we imagined we'd ride out the gale
in high style — has splintered and sunk,
one gunwale washed onto the beach
for the jittery, pea-brained seagulls to perch on
and spatter. What does that matter,
the angel asks. One rib made the world once.

LEISURAMA

A dog barks. Around the cul-de-sac,
a man pounds shingles onto a roof,
sound of a solid home. Dad,
you said I'd find God
while doing laundry. Yes, I miss
a roof. I miss how the sea sounds,
the yarrow smell of sheets
pinned to a summer line.
So far, so fine, I haven't done
much laundry, nor found God,
or is it He who hasn't
finished finding me?

FOR MY FATHER ON HIS BIRTHDAY

How have you made the sickle
a symbol of regeneration?
In your hands the scythe, the sign
of death, is transformed.

Perhaps it is the too-short shorts
instead of a black habit,
or that you are unmasked—

A man tanning his gently worn hide,
face tipped beneath an elder's hat,
as your St. Christopher dangles down
toward the last tall grass.

The rest of the tonsured field
rejoices in what it has lost.

PURE

My mother keeps bees on the terrace
in violation of the city code. They please her
with their constant work. Last spring,
her bees were born wingless.
They dragged their polished bodies
through the pewter wax
for maybe a day, and died.
Now woe betide the mites who invade
her hive. Eyeing her shelved city,
she plots a genocide.

BERRY PICKING

There are moments, Mother, when you sleep
that the dreams you keep to yourself
play out around your beautiful mouth.
I see you from the backside picking berries,
the simple, ample bowl drips in the sink,
the clink of ice and the clean fizz of gin—
the juniper smell at the vesper end of day.
The Lord gives, He takes away—
what would you say He took from you?

To bless means to wound.
To wound means to mark as one's own.

There are people, Mother,
who don't know God
and float around equally loved.

We are workers, you and I,
too busy with our hands
to look up much.

DIVORCE

Red bucket and clogs,
the way the wave lightens
as it crests. The rest
of the water's dull weight
falls away and just this
glass lip lifts itself
or is lifted. Sand sifts
through the child's screen.
She will remember
mother and father
digging past
the waterline
when any depth
seemed possible.

EPITHALAMION

That accursed island in the fog—
the borrowed pomp of bagpipes—
no, I don't think you'd dare.
Your new wife's hair is terrible,
you know. The dress, of course, is white,
a life wiped clean. Everything is fake
except the rock. Forgive me
all my pettiness. Love contracted once
is double-bound to pain.
I wish you every happiness.
I hope it rains.

CLEAN

On the western ghats of the city,
children are bathing,
husbands are burning their wives.
The river, resigned, takes everyone in.

Some say the river is bent on death,
but we are born with murder at the caul;
crowned with what's been torn
from our mother,

squatting to wash the pits of herself
with one hand pure enough to serve
the body's high and public needs,
the nether other shunned and still.

FOREIGN CORRESPONDENCE

A child coughs from beneath a roof
of pirated tin. The radio chuckles
in French from the coast
where the room is cool
and someone is wearing a tie.
The walls are thinner here.
I wake to the sound of a man
beating his wife.

BORDER BALLAD

In camp, the one pump works all night
and starved cows jostle for the overflow.
They low to each other in the dark
to determine who and how many
have vanished at the camp's edge.
No one keeps count of the children
as they whistle in deep grass
to the slosh of their fetched water
and to another sound—half-noticed,
never understood. If they scream
they scream like rabbits—
that high, defeated wail
left useless in the grass
beside their emptied pail.

MONKEY

The soldiers are children and the monkey's young.
He clings to my leg, heart against calf—
a throat filling, refilling with blood.
Last week, the children ate his mother—
dashed her head against the breadfruit.
A young girl soldier laughs,
tears the baby from my leg
and hurls him toward the tree.
See, she says, you have to be rough.
When she was taken, the girl's
heart too pulsed in her throat.

BATS

We met beneath a black-leafed tree.
It was hot. The leaves rustled
but there was no wind, only sun.
See that one? You lifted
your non-smoking hand
toward a branch. The black leaves
were bat wings and below,
their petrified droppings
spattered scattershot:
an aerial of Old Jerusalem.
Carriers, you said.
This was years before I left you
near dead with that dazzling fever.
Alive, we slept on everything
but beds—church pews, school benches,
smashed glass, car seats, mud.
We laughed until our noses bled.

DRODRO

Death isn't beautiful.
It isn't anything.
It smells sometimes.
At night, we tell stories against it.
We sing and drink
communion wine,
screwing off
the foil top
with our teeth
and tossing it at God.

OCCUPATION

The prostitutes in Kabul tap their feet
beneath their faded burqas in the heat.

For bread or fifteen cents, they'll take a man to bed—
their husbands dead, their seven kids unfed—

and thanks to occupation, rents have risen twentyfold,
their chickens, pots and carpets have been sold.

Two years ago, the Talibs favored boys and left the girls alone.
A woman then was worth her weight in stone.

The Uzbek boys on Chicken Street
have never had enough to eat.
They stock from shelf to shining shelf
these GI meals, which boil themselves
in added water (bottled, please).
In twenty minutes, processed cheese
on jambalaya followed by
a peanut butter jamboree.

The boys, polite,
advise on which we might prefer—
Beef Teriyaki, Turkey Blight—
and thank us twice for bringing peace
as, meals in hand, we leave the store.
Of course they know that any peace
that must be kept by force
goes by another name.

MINE

A red-feathered bird on a fence post;
and behind the barbed garland
a petrified shoe: mouth agape,
tongue lolling. The wind is a cripple
who peers beneath tufts of white grasses
and herds invisible sheep
toward this patch of planted field
into which we have already wandered —
both of us prone to explode.

Now do what again? Follow
the tank treads; avoid disturbed earth.
The concertina hums her impersonal dirge.
"If you blow your leg off," you say,
in your charming, rheumy-eyed way,
"I'll leave you. I'm supposed to."

You must have learned this on your course:
minimize the loss, drop to your belly
and crawl toward the gate. I take
the first forced step away and wait.

A LONGER GOODBYE

The bedside table unpacked:
pink-eye salve and eczema lotion,
two fingers of ouzo, the Libyan pistol
for which you were frisked in the lobby.
In the background, the sound of the shower.
Less than an hour till leaving.
Now there is only steam
and small grieving. The rest of you packed.
My mess is strewn over the floor
and the chair. No more affair.

TRANSIT

You woke up feeling
for your gun's false safety
but they'd taken your gun
in another country
where they took me
and you were left with your
guilt and your gut rot
and a picture in your wallet
of another man's child.

FAIRYTALE

The promise was to forget each other
or you forget me and return
to the forsaken cottage
whitewashed with fresh lye.
How are you faring
in real life?
Have the Gypsies come back
to the window? Beware
the fiery one with the tiny feet.
She'll eat your heart out.
She'll be the first
me after me —
at least you have your pretty lake,
your rock wall, your pile
of wood waiting to be quartered
and severed from itself.

COME AND SEE

You said it, Seamus, marching down
the grizzled ridge while the boy
collected dshka shells in a helmet
he held by the chin strap,
like Easter. Everywhere
was mined and so much mud.
Downtown a Syrian sat on the curb;
his captors stood by, watched us,
waited for us to leave. You knew what
that first black hood meant,
hailed a makeshift ambulance.
The man was lifted from the curb alive
at least until the white doors shut.

AUTHORITY

The flaming city makes it rain.
The siege has changed the weather.
We lie together on the luggage:
the generator that won't work,
a poisoned rice sack.
This is so many years ago
and fifteen seconds.
I'm embarrassed to remember
the time before I grew
uncertain about you,
or that I had a right to say
where I had been
and what I saw there.

HOW TO

On the cliff you've just left
a puff of snow rings like smoke.
I didn't know snow did that.
Nor that a man could fling
himself from such a height
and mean to land alive.
Soon, in love's descent
I will learn to drag
this image from my screen.
You, against your will,
how to survive.

Only today did I think of your gear:
chalk bags, cam lube, harness, friends —
all lying about taking care. You play
with death up there; the good kid's hit,
risk's cheap high, like whippets,
except you've never done whippets,
and neither have I. You gasp at the welts
on my back left by Congolese fleas
as if my job were an affliction.
Look at yourself on your knees
in the most beautiful place in the world,
craving fear. That's addiction.

LITHIUM

The hospital has six beds
of butterfly weed and you
tucked into your dreams
like a tuber wintering out.

So what you've seen the world end—
who else has licked God's palm
and been cured by salt.

LOVE

The dead bird you brought me,
head tucked under wing,
is proof, you say. I can't tell
if you had a hand in her death,
or does a deeper comfort
come from holding her.

ROUGH

Not you, with your elite heart,
pink-valved, its chambers pure
if clinging to the air. What I never told you
came before. I thought I'd had enough.
You were the antidote.
It wasn't enough.

STROKE

Charlie was the emperor of summer,
roaring down the dirt road to the dump
on his tomato tractor; felt hat
for a helmet, devouring smile,
he terrified me twenty years ago.
Since last year, half his body works;
his smile's now half a mouth's apology.
A bird bangs into the gable he built,
a stunning error. He leaves the tractor
in our lower field; he cannot shift the gears.
From a window, I watch his son work a backhoe
lifting Charlie's manhood in its mouth.

FORGIVENESS

I already owe you.
Rage has more velocity than pain.
To think of you again,
how good it could have been
had we been slightly different
at a slightly different angle of the day.
It doesn't work this way.

WINTER

Let the sound of snow underfoot
no longer remind me
of you tugging Grace
across the pasture,
dogs hitched to the flying saucer,
panting, of all I could not sustain
as the snow lay round about
coating the brittle grass
with its lovely white lie.

TIGERS

What are we now but voices
who promise each other a life
neither one can deliver
not for lack of wanting
but wanting won't make it so.
We cling to a vine
at the cliff's edge.
There are tigers above
and below. Let us love
one another and let go.

COPPER

In the old quarter I pass boys sniffing glue,
cuff to mouth, teeth carved with the habit.
Their brains drool through their noses.
Across the world, a bomb goes off and you say,
See what happens in the city you dream of?
I nod through the stripped line
and don't say, No, this *is* what I dream.
When are you coming back, you ask.
I ask myself. If I said never what would you do.

HAZARD

Last night a drunk Finn drowned.
The sand pyre made for him
and the votives' hardened puddles
are more beautiful
than he was.

At the bar, one of his friends,
eyes pied with whatever drove
the dead man into the riptide,
absinthe maybe, squats and asks
how much for the night.

This morning a boy stands under the sun,
the light so deceptively bright
his grimace seems like happiness.
His mother licks his skin to see
if he's been in yet; then he wades
toward the break.

BEDBUGS

In the Bedouin's foam mattress,
a bedbug mother tips back her baby's chin
and pours my blood down his throat. You wrote
in all my wandering I risk my chance
to give birth. That's hardly true. All over
the earth, I've fed my flesh to bugs.
That's some kind of mother for you.

RETREAT

The city abandoned; its citizens fled.
A paper chain hung on the wall left standing.
A single flip-flop graced the hardpacked floor.
The rest diminishes their loss: these were barracks,
and yesterday the men tried to blow a hole
through me as I squatted up the road
and took note of their grim frenzy,
like termites, no, more like tiny sailors
from a different time, when war came
over water and the battle arrived at a delay.
There was nothing to do but watch the enemy
grow from blot to galleon; colors nailed
to the mast. Like the bright orange flashing
we hung on our car's hood that said to the sky,
Don't bomb us, we are your friends.
These others, they had no friends in the sky.

WATER CURE

Before drowning, after the gasp
when firefly lights pop and sputter
around the prisoner's eyes:
this is the line to recognize.
The manual recommends a pause
to let the man confess.
If there is no water and you must press on,
then strip him naked. After the shock,
watch him watch the fake-out clock and realize
the hours are yours to stretch against him.
Shock, or better, dunk again.
Try self-inflicted pain.

HAYAT

We could judge him
because who did he think he was,
handing his daughter to a stranger to hold,
sharing his wife's one pair of shoes,
telling the same truth to governments, gunmen
without fearing who listened.
These days you don't do that.
We are sad for a second.
He would have been a hero had he lived.

DEVI

When no one was looking
I hurled my half an apple
into the street. You said,
Don't eat the skin.
Below us, a crowd gathered
to play their new drum.
I was terrified. Why did you
bring me here to leave me
with more questions?
How do they make a flute
out of a dead boy's femur?
What did the goddess say
when we sat before her,
knees touching? She laughed,
you didn't translate.

NEPALGUNJ

It costs three cents to cross.
The boatman's teenage son stays on the bank.
Sometimes he shepherds, other times
he shrugs and shakes his head.
What stops him — is it my shell
of predictable ambitions, shaking
my purse of worries like a bag of teeth?
The boat pulls against its tether
like a colt wanting loose on the river.

AT THE KING DAVID

We fight about paradise
because it's easier
than asking each other
how far we'll go.

The secret is nothing divides us.

Beneath us, tomorrow's dead
dig against darkness,
their heads bent as ours are
in the universal work of survival—
one spoonful of dirt at a time—
hoping that as they inch forward
what they displace won't cause
the roof to collapse,
until it does.

LEAVING THE VALLEY

The quince-colored smear
of first light, the dove of mud and rubble,
the scrap of frock, torn
in mourning and tied to a grave,
will blow away.
What would feed your eye?
The mountains are the mystery,
what is withheld and why.

ARREST

The joins in the highway rise below the tires
as if we are running over bodies.
The windows are covered in butcher paper
and night coming cools the car's frame.
My head hangs the way cows' do:
complete submission to being led.
The last thing I saw was the red cloth coming
before it was tied around my eyes.
My spirit thumps in the darkness.
I've seen the pictures on the internet.
Sometimes I fake a swoon or cry,
hoping it might free me.
Sometimes I refuse to answer
questions they already know.
They feed me water from a cup;
I swallow. How human we are,
the tender, puncturing skin,
the illusion we can save ourselves
if we find the right words
and try with all our might.

THE POLITICS OF DREAMS

The hooded men run
through the daytime streets,
anonymous, wreaking
havoc—the hoods
designed to contain them
can be seen out of but not
into, like smoked glass.
They are against us
and to save ourselves
we string them by the dozen
upside down—hooded,
trussed and writhing.
Some die, which is a relief.
After the hanging, there's
no letting them go.
You asked me what I dreamt of.
Now you know.

CONCRETE

I hate coming home.
The delis depress me.
I try to remember
this city is not horizontal.
The stacked hungers
are what matters.

ACTING

I now know the value
of physical business:
give the dumb girl
something to do with her hands
so no one looks at her face.

COLLECT

Did you, as a boy, once pray
for water's buffer?

Something viscous and clear
to slow those who came
near your boy's body
to show themselves
they existed.

In your pens' perfect worlds
every landing is liquid.
Hong Kong slides
from side to side.
Your helicopter
never drops its A.

As a man you've made
your mind one
no one can get
through, even you.

SO

Like a night-blooming cereus
or any other bud that shuts
at daybreak to save itself,
I feel my heart closing.
It's not enough to feel this;
I have to try, at least,
to figure out why.
Let's start with the sun,
what is it then —
the cold hard knowledge
we're alone, or a bid
to go on? Who can tell me,
and if there's no who,
how can I know?

OCTOBER

The chairs have come in
and the crisp yellow thwock
of the ball being hit
says somehow, now that it's fall,
I'm a memory of myself.
My whole old life—
I mourn you sometimes
in places you would have been.

BEYOND THE SOLACE OF A
DEVASTATED LANDSCAPE

You don't need a war.
You don't need to go anywhere.
It's a myth: if you hurl
yourself at chaos
chaos will catch you.

POWWOW

Having made peace with the usual demons,
the characters at my mind's powwow
sit awkward around the table.
Each archetype checks himself
before commenting on the weather—
there's nothing else to say.
They search for shared experience,
can't find it, break up early,
go home to kiss their wives.

EVOLUTION

Was it dissatisfaction or hope
that beckoned some of the monkeys
down from the trees and onto the damp
forbidden musk of the forest floor?

Which one tested his thumbs
against the twig
and awkwardly dug a grub
from the soil?

What did the tribe above think
as it leaned on the slender branches
watching the others
frustrated, embarrassed,
but pinching grubs
with leathery fingers
into their mouths?

The moral is movement
is awkward. The lesson is fumble.

MODERN CITY

A wedge of steel flung skyward
and beyond it the prairie flatlines.
Each unhappy family permits itself
another slice of pie. The sky turns
constantly trying to get it right.
To the east, the slum eats itself:
a man in satin fields calls
and sells on the children's block.
To the west, the west begins.
Beneath us in the underground museum
moths feed at the stuffed muskrat
and the grizzly's fur fades to white,
so white you argue he's a different bear.

CALIFORNIA

My best friend grows kumquats
and something deadly on a vine.
I am in love with a man who believes
he's a minefield. I see him more
like that high-windowed room
in *Hotel New Hampshire*.
Who was it, Freud, who said
if given half a chance
we'd lift our little feet
and do-si-do right off the sill.

AUBADE

I wake to the smell of a stranger's toast
and a knocking so bad in my pipes
I can't believe I slept through.
It's air, I know,
but it sounds like someone begging out.
The nightmares have returned.
I circle the airport.
You recede.

WHAT WENT WRONG

Again then, disintegration,
like paper in water.

I once drowned a passport
to dissolve an image the match hadn't.

We handle each other
with too much gentleness,
like eggs,
to be born elsewhere and later.

STATION

In another state, snow falls and downstairs,
a colt of a woman laughs into the cordless.
Her older, more difficult self
laughs back, though I can't hear.
True intelligence is boundlessly generous.
That's why, as you and I reach this sad station,
I open my hands and find in their emptiness
a deeper appreciation of who you are
regardless of me.

HOPE

I see you again across the sparse grass,
you who were gone, waving your arms
like fiery wings. I raise my hand
against the glare to be sure of you.
To be sure means the reopened question,
the unclenched heart asking what now.

WIDEAWAKE FIELD

I've never been where we are,
although the grass studded
with soldiers' rusted buttons
says we aren't the first.
The airstrip's islands of cracked macadam
suggest an ancient volcano.
We are the volcano.
We, the notes sung
by a creator, who, if not singular,
is creation—
not an idea, a force.
Let us tumble.
Let us laugh at our grip.
If these are last days,
let them not catch us sleeping
but awake in this field, and ready.

In "Sadness," the phrase "doubled in the water" comes from a poem of the same name by Donald Justice.

+

"Leisurama" refers to a 1960s prefabricated house first built in Moscow, then reconstructed at Macy's, New York. The Leisurama sold for $12,995, including toothbrushes. Many were built on Montauk Point, at the eastern end of Long Island.

+

The water cure is a form of torture, also known as the question, used by the French during the seventeenth and eighteenth centuries. During the "ordinary question," an interrogator forced eight pints of water into the stomach; during the "extraordinary question," sixteen pints. The United States currently employs a variant called waterboarding, first used during the Philippine-American War and described by Lieutenant Grover Flint as:

> A man is thrown down on his back and three or four men sit or
> stand on his arms and legs and hold him down; and either a gun
> barrel or a rifle barrel or a carbine barrel or a stick as big as a be-
> laying pin,—that is, with an inch circumference,—is simply
> thrust into his jaws and his jaws are thrust back, and, if possible,

a wooden log or stone is put under his head or neck, so he can be held more firmly. In the case of very old men I have seen their teeth fall out,—I mean when it was done a little roughly. He is simply held down and then water is poured onto his face down his throat and nose from a jar; and that is kept up until the man gives some sign or becomes unconscious. And, when he becomes unconscious, he is simply rolled aside and he is allowed to come to. In almost every case the men have been a little roughly handled. They were rolled aside rudely, so that water was expelled. A man suffers tremendously, there is no doubt about it. His sufferings must be that of a man who is drowning, but cannot drown. (Quoted by Stuart Creighton Mill in *"Benevolent Assimilation": The American Conquest of the Philippines, 1899–1903*)

+

Wideawake Field is the name of an airstrip built by the United States on Ascension Island during World War II. From 1943 to 1945, it was used in more than twenty thousand missions to the Middle Eastern, African, and European theaters of war.